J

CONTEMPORARY
TURNED WOOD

*New
Perspectives
in a Rich
Tradition*

RAY LEIER · JAN PETERS · KEVIN WALLACE

CONTEMPORARY
TURNED WOOD

New

Perspectives

in a Rich

Tradition

Hand Books Press, Madison, Wisconsin

Distributed by Popular Woodworking Books, Cincinnati, Ohio

FRONT COVER ARTWORK:
William Hunter, *Kinetic Rhythms 33*,
cocobolo, 7"H x 11"Dia, photo: Hap Sakwa.

BACK COVER ARTWORK:
(top) Bob Stocksdale, untitled bowl,
Pacific yew, 3¹/₄"H x 4³/₄"Dia;
(center) Hans Weissflog, *Rocking Bowl*,
bocote, 4"H x 6¹/₂"Dia;
(bottom) Robyn Horn, *Slashed Millstone*,
ebonized redwood burl, 22"H x 20"W x 8"D,
photo: George Chambers.

TITLE PAGE ARTWORK:
Michael Hosaluk, *Traveling Bowl*, sassafras,
linen thread and found objects, 4"H x 8"Dia,
photo: Grant Kernan.

THIS PAGE:
James Prestini, untitled bowl, mahogany,
2"H x 7"Dia, photo: George Chambers.

CONTEMPORARY TURNED WOOD
Ray Leier
Jan Peters
Kevin Wallace

© Copyright 1999 by Hand Books Press

Primary photography: David Peters
Design: Stephen Bridges and Laura Herrmann
Editor: Katie Kazan
Editorial Assistants: Robert E. Winters, Nikki Muenchow

03 02 01 00 99   5 4 3 2 1

Published by
Hand Books Press, a joint venture of
THE GUILD and Design Books International
931 E. Main Street #106
Madison, WI 53703 USA
TEL 608-256-1990 • TEL 800-969-1556 • FAX 608-256-1938

Distributed by Popular Woodworking Books
An imprint of F&W Publications, Inc.
1507 Dana Avenue • Cincinnati, OH 45207
TEL 513-531-2222 • TEL 800-289-0963

Printed in China

ISBN 0-9658248-8-8

TABLE OF CONTENTS

ARTIST: William Moore
TITLE: Celebes
MATERIALS: Copper, koa and maple
DIMENSIONS: 16"H x 21½"W x 7"D

INTRODUCTION

Take a moment to look at the piece on the cover of this book. Ask yourself: "Is it a work of art?" Created by master wood-turner William Hunter, **Kinetic Weave 33** is a sculpture of superb craftsmanship. It draws the eye in and along a journey of exploration, around and into the surface and interior of the piece. There is a purity to the artist's statement. The spiral, a recurrent theme in Hunter's work, speaks of his fascination with motion and interplay.

The question of whether or not this is a work of art is an important one, as the medium of turned wood has just recently begun to gain acceptance as an art form. When turned wood bowls and vessels began to transcend function, the field began to be accepted as a decorative art. Initially, the aesthetic was a simple one of natural beauty and line, and the work did not aspire to say anything beyond. William Hunter epitomizes the spirit of the artists who have taken turned wood to new levels. Not satisfied with creating purely functional pieces or production work, these artists have struck out on their own, developing highly personal bodies of work. In so doing, they have created a 20th-century art form.

The pages which follow tell the story of these artists and show examples of the finest work being created today. Is it art? Emphatically, yes! The criteria traditionally used to evaluate art confirms that conclusion. Growing from roots of tradition, turned wood today is bold and exciting, charged with beauty and unique vision. The work of these artists, viewed in its historical context, will surely stand the test of time.

A HISTORY OF THE CONTEMPORARY WOOD STUDIO MOVEMENT

To understand the current state of contemporary wood, one must consider those master woodturners who pioneered the medium, taking it from its history of utilitarian bowls into the realm of art. They created the techniques and determined the aesthetic standards that set the stage for today's artists. The history of the field is the story of these individuals and their unique approaches to the medium.

James Prestini, a Bauhaus-influenced professor, engineer and sculptor, can be credited with creating the field of turned wood as we know it today. Between the years 1933 and 1953, he created a large body of work which woodturner David Ellsworth has described as "... objects of incomparable elegance and grace, objects which spoke about the synthesis of form, function,

proportion and scale."[1] Concentrating on straight-grained woods, as opposed to burls or exotics, Prestini was the first to create pure wood forms which transcended utility, thin bowls which had more in common with historical glass and ceramics than previous woodturning. Presented in a major exhibition at the Museum of Modern Art in 1949, the work of Prestini established the validity of the wood bowl as an object of art.

ABOVE: James Prestini, untitled bowl, maple, 2"H x 12½"Dia. Presented in a major exhibition at the Museum of Modern Art in 1949, the work of Prestini established the validity of the wood bowl as an object of art. Most of the artist's works now reside in museum collections.

OPPOSITE: Mark Lindquist, *Chieftains' Bowl*, spalted maple burl, 25½"H x 17"Dia, collection: Fuller Museum of Art, MA. The Metropolitan Museum's 1978 acquisition of work by Mark Lindquist and his father Melvin Lindquist marked early recognition for this important work.

ONE

1. *Woodturning Magazine*, Summer 1991, page 41.

Bob Stocksdale, untitled bowl, macadamia, 4¹/₄"H x 4³/₄"Dia. Rather than making a personal statement by creating a form unlike any other, Stocksdale's focus has always been on the quality of the single turned bowl. The artist chooses forms which best display the unusual grains and colors of exotic woods from around the world, sometimes altering the initial design to eliminate a flaw or take advantage of an opportunity in a piece of wood.

Melvin Lindquist, *Geometric Series Vase*, buckeye burl, 14"H x 8"Dia. Lindquist uses his engineering experience to advance his own natural curiosity and his study of Greek, Oriental and Native American ceramics to broaden his artistic sensibilities.

Photo: Randy Lovoy

Ed Moulthrop, *Ashleaf Maple Chalice*, ashleaf maple (acer negundo), 23"H x 20"Dia. Moulthrop believes that each bowl already exists in the trunk of the tree and that "...one's job is simply to uncover it and somehow chip away the excess wood, much as you would chip away the surrounding stone to uncover a perfect fossil entombed in the stone."

Photo: Paul G. Beswick

Over the two decades when Prestini was creating his celebrated bowl forms, four other artists began to produce work which would have a lasting impact on the field. These progenitors include a farmer's son from the Midwest, who turned his first bowl in a camp for conscientious objectors; an engineer for General Electric Company on the East Coast, who experimented from his home woodshop; a teacher living in the mountains of Kentucky, who created functional turned pieces to earn extra income; and an architect from the South, who bought his first lathe as a teenager, with money earned delivering magazines. These four figures were unaware or uninfluenced by the work being done by Prestini or one another. Each made significant breakthroughs and contributions to the field.

Bob Stocksdale, a major influence on the field, began to repair furniture as a teenager living on his parents' farm in Indiana. Working without electricity, he turned table legs using a gas-powered washing machine motor to power a lathe. Drafted following the 1941 attack on Pearl Harbor and feeling that war "never solved anything," he ended up in a camp for conscientious objectors, where he turned his first bowl.

Work by Stocksdale came to reflect the influence of tea bowls from the Far East. Acknowledging this, he says with a smile, "The Chinese have been borrowing my forms for two thousand years." In the case of Stocksdale's work, the grain and figure of the wood replaced the designs provided by raku, wood-firing or glaze in ceramic. Rather than concerning himself with making a personal statement by using unusual forms, Stocksdale has always focused on creating individual bowls which best display the unusual grains and colors of exotic woods.

Living in the relative isolation of the rural mountains of Kentucky, Rude Osolnik also began turning wood in the 1940s. Creating work which often reflected the traditions of southern folk crafts, he soon began to rethink some of those traditions and develop innovative new approaches. Osolnik's experimentation with veneers and irregular cast-off woods opened the way for others to explore the possibilities. Although he left his teaching position at

Berea College in the 1950s to devote full time to turning wood, he has continued to this day to reach out to students and other artists through workshops, conferences and demonstrations across the country.

Melvin Lindquist, trained as an engineer, began turning in the 1930s as a vertical turret-lathe operator for the General Electric Company. On weekends in his home workshop, he began turning wood foraged from the forest around his cabin in the Adirondack Mountains. He developed methods of blind boring and reverse turning, and thus paved the way for artists to create hollow vessels and forms with narrow neck openings. Intrigued by spalted and decayed wood, previously considered useless to woodworkers, he is credited with the first serious exploration of this exotic and delicate material, expanding the idea of what sort of wood is aesthetically attractive.

Ed Moulthrop has been turning wood since he was 15 years old. While working as a successful architect in the 1960s, he began creating the monumental pieces for which he is best known. By the mid-70s he was a full-time turner, dedicated to using only local southern woods. He pioneered the use of chemical stabilizers to create increasingly larger pieces, and developed his trademark finish to best reveal the myriad range of colors and patterns in the wood. By employing only simple shapes and forms to display the natural beauty of the wood without distracting from it, Moulthrop creates minimalist sculpture.

Working independently, these early pioneers developed their own styles, tools and philosophies about turned wood objects. Their work provided a revelation and a starting point for a new generation of woodturners. Artists such as Mark Lindquist, David Ellsworth, Giles Gilson and William Hunter built upon this foundation, each adding their own innovations to an expanding field.

Mark Lindquist began turning early in life, working with his father Melvin Lindquist, but his interest led him first into music, then into art. He studied sculpture in college and graduate school, working in metal, stone and ceramics. As a potter's apprentice, he

Rude Osolnik, *Candlesticks,* tulipwood, from 3¹/₂" to 16"H. Osolnik's philosophy is not far removed from the artists of the Bauhaus, who taught that the objects we use daily should heighten our visual sensitivity. "If you've got a set of candleholders on the dining room table, you're going to be arranging them every day," he explains. "If it's a nice design, you're going to be much more conscious of form and shape in everything else."

Photo: Rick Siciliano

BELOW: William Hunter, *Kinetic Diamonds,* cocobolo, 13¹/₂"H x 6"Dia. "When designing my work, from a vessel adorned only by the brush stroke of nature to the most complex carved and constructed pieces, I try always to give each piece its own rich but single voice."

Photo: Hap Sakwa

ABOVE LEFT: Giles Gilson, *The Maker,* curly maple, purpleheart, walnut, holly, East Indian rosewood, paduak, birch, cocobolo, dyed veneer, brass, corian and lacquer, 16¹/₂"H x 6¹/₄"Dia. "I really believe that the work is the person and the person is the work; that they are one and the same," Gilson explains. "An artist's work represents that person and the circumstances that were in existence at the time the piece was created."

Photo: George Chambers

Del Stubbs, *Fairy Goblets,* madrone, 4¹/₄"H x 1"Dia, 5¹/₈"H x 1¹/₂"Dia and 4¹/₄"H x 1"Dia. Having set a high standard for those who have followed, Del Stubbs has shared his ideas and techniques with the woodturning community.

David Ellsworth, *Homage Pot #8,* spalted maple, 8¹/₂"H x 6"Dia. Utilizing a process called "blind turning," David Ellsworth hollows vessels from a small opening guided entirely by touch and sound, rather than sight.

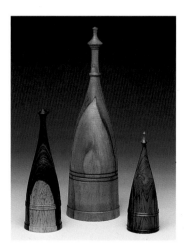

Richard Raffan, *Tower Series Boxes,* (left to right) cocobolo, 6"H x 2"D, Tasmanian blackwood, 10"H x 3"Dia, cocobolo, 5"H x 1¹/₂"Dia. These architectural box forms have threaded lids. Australian author and woodturner Richard Raffan has traveled extensively as a teacher, and has been described as a woodturning evangelist. Thousands can credit Raffan's books as an important part of their education.

Dale Nish, *Nagare Vessel,* bleached wormy ash, 3¹/₂"H x 5³/₄"W x 5"D. Many woodturners credit the books of Dale Nish for their education in woodturning. He has also been a driving force behind the annual symposium on woodturning held at Brigham Young University in Utah.

explored ancient and contemporary ceramics of many cultures. When he returned to wood, he brought all these influences to his work. Transcending previous limitations in the field, Mark Lindquist's wood sculpture introduced ideas and statements more common to contemporary art than turned wood at the time. He applied the forms and philosophy of significant art historical periods to woodturning and developed radical new techniques and aesthetics for the turned bowl.

David Ellsworth has credited the quality of Bob Stocksdale's work, the power and scale of Ed Moulthrop's work and the inventiveness of the Lindquists' work with inspiring him. A generation of woodturners credit David Ellsworth with taking the hollow vessel beyond the accepted limitations. Influenced by ceramics and the fine arts, Ellsworth is known for his technical ability and understanding of form, as well as his exploration of the vessel as sculptural statement.

Giles Gilson protests against the restrictions of the medium. "Does it have to be turned?" he asks. "Does it have to be wood?" A leader of the field's avant-garde artists, Gilson has been responsible for introducing paint and mixed-media approaches to the turned wood form, and creating segmented wood forms as early as the mid-70s. Never satisfied to repeat himself, the artist pushes ahead relentlessly, shocking purist enthusiasts and remaining at the forefront of the field.

William Hunter began turning wood in 1969. Although his early work was primarily sculpted tobacco pipes and decorative wood pieces, he soon devoted himself to the exploration of the sculptural form. Hunter is fascinated with the spiral, as it seems to emulate the motion of the lathe. Considered an innovator in the field, he was among the first to employ various attachments and use the lathe as a carving tool to create the flutes and undulating surfaces of his pieces. His uncompromising techniques and use of exotic hardwoods have set a standard of sophistication and excellence for future generations of woodturners.

Artists in the field of turned wood have often worked in isolation and without the advantage of communication with each other. Skills and techniques were developed independently, leading to unorthodox approaches and experimentation. In the mid-70s Albert LeCoff and Palmer Sharpless began organizing woodturning symposiums designed to bring woodworkers together to share experiences and advance the field. These symposiums eventually led to the formation of The Wood Turning Center in 1985. This nonprofit arts institution has become an important component for exposing the work of woodturners through traveling exhibitions, publications and special educational programs.

Del Stubbs, who credits these early symposiums with creating a much needed sense of community among woodturners, soon found himself much in demand in a rapidly expanding field. Known for technical accomplishments such as turning paper-thin bowl forms and creating precision-fitted boxes, the artist found more satisfaction in creating objects of subtle beauty. This desire,

coupled with his desire to explore his abilities as a craftsperson, has led him to travel the world and work with artists and craftspeople from all walks of life.

In 1986, the American Association of Woodturners was established. Although it began with only a handful of woodturners, it now boasts more than 5,000 members worldwide and has become an important forum for the advancement of the field. The AAW's monthly periodical *American Woodturner* has provided valuable documentation and given inspiration to its membership. The annual symposiums sponsored by the organization feature demonstration workshops by leading turners, including David Ellsworth, John Jordan, Ron Kent, Bruce Mitchell, Christian Burchard and Al Stirt. They have proven to be catalysts for the rapid expansion of the woodturning movement. In the international arena, Stephen Hogbin from Canada, Dale Nish from the United States and Richard Raffan from Australia have increased awareness through their instructional books as well as their traveling workshops.

Stephen Hogbin, untitled, walnut, 18¹/₄"H x 11"W x 7"D. Canadian Stephen Hogbin is the author of *Woodturning: The Purpose of the Object.* As craftsman-in-residence at the Victorian State College in Australia in the mid-1970s, he was a driving force, inspiring Australian artists to appreciate and explore native timbers.

John Jordan, *Ebonized Vase,* dyed and carved maple, 6"H x 7"Dia. "The pieces I make are simple but finely detailed vessels," Jordan explains. "Manipulating the color and patterns in the wood to complement the form is an important part of the process."

Ron Kent, untitled bowl, Norfolk Island pine, 12"H x 12¹/₂"Dia. Ron Kent's initial challenge is to uncover the natural beauty in the log, which he works to bring out in the most appealing silhouette for presenting the grain, knots and coloration. "Originality and virtuosity are important only if, and as, they enhance the natural beauty of the wood," he explains.

Ron Fleming, *Andora*, mahogany, 15½"H x 13"Dia. "I love nature," Fleming says. "Each piece gives me a way to express my feelings about the things I see around me and to share these visions with others."

Todd Hoyer, *Ringed Series*, cottonwood and wire, 12"H x 7"Dia. The wood in this piece has been weathered and wrapped with rusted wire to reflect the passage of time and the aging process.

Stoney Lamar, *Torso*, madrone, 19"H x 16"W x 6"D. Stoney Lamar uses the lathe primarily as a carving tool, using multi-axis techniques to create sculptural statements.

Robyn Horn, *Graven Image IV*, madrone burl, 19½"H x 12½"W x 13"D. "One of the main attractions to wood is its warmth and beauty," says Robyn Horn. "With this as a preliminary basis, my approach to sculpture has been an effort to combine shape and form with movement in varying geometric abstract shapes."

Photo: George Chambers

Among the artists who have been generous with sharing their breakthroughs and individual techniques are John Jordan and Ron Kent. While elevating the quality of bowl and vessel forms, this openness can bring with it the dubious distinction of being flattered by imitation.

John Jordan has introduced surface textures which change the appearance of the wood. Creating variations on classical forms, he uses a variety of carving techniques, occasionally bleaching or dyeing the wood to achieve an objective.

Through the development of the technique of oil-soaking his Norfolk Island pine bowls, Ron Kent has added an element not usually associated with wood: light. His bowls glow with a translucent quality, and by inducing and controlling the effects of spalting, he has been able to exploit the natural patterns in the wood. The resulting bowl has an aesthetic which is classical, minimal and concerned with beauty.

While many artists have refined and explored the vessel form, others have sought to transform it. Through carving, Michelle Holzapfel expresses conceptual and narrative elements within the framework of the vessel. Ron Fleming brings his experience as an illustrator and his love of nature to the motifs he employs.

Lamination and segmentation are other techniques woodturners are using to accomplish their artistic goals. Virginia Dotson, Bud Latven, Ray Allen and Michael Shuler have each mastered the material and use construction to manipulate color and pattern in their distinctly individual bodies of work.

Still others, such as Todd Hoyer and Michael Peterson, may occasionally allude to the vessel form but have moved beyond it. Todd Hoyer's interest in archaeological objects is obvious in his work. He embraces characteristics like cracking and insect damage, adding weathering and burning to make autobiographical statements.

Michael Peterson creates work which seems fossilized by sandblasting, bleaching, burnishing and carving. While many artists are influenced by forms from diverse civilizations, Peterson looks to his surroundings: the shapes and textures of driftwood on the beach, rock formations on the local hillside or the grace of a bird in flight.

Leaving the vessel form completely, Stoney Lamar and Robyn Horn set themselves apart early in their careers by creating purely sculptural work utilizing the lathe. Increasingly, collectors and curators have come to embrace sculptural statements by contemporary turned wood artists.

Support by the visionary collectors who recognized the potential of this once underappreciated field — and the gallery owners and curators who arranged exhibitions of the work long before it was accepted — has been crucial. But it has been the pioneering artists, experimenting in a medium of unexplored potential, who are at the heart of this movement. This spirit of exploration and experimentation continues today.

Michael Peterson, *Arroyo (Landscape Series)*, locust burl, turned, carved, sandblasted and bleached, 5"H x 12"Dia. "*Arroyo* expresses my passion for landscape and my appreciation of the vessel form," says Michael Peterson. "Allowing one to emerge from the other seemed the natural thing to do. I never tire of celebrating the creative energy I find within this series."

Michelle Holzapfel, *Cushioned Bowl II*, curly sugar maple, 6"H x 16"Dia. Michelle Holzapfel says *Cushioned Bowl II* originated from her desire to "give shape to the quiet heroism of the domestic realm, to illustrate and illuminate the hard-earned nobility of 'home' through visual narrative, using motifs of weaving, sewing, braiding, enclosing and layering."

ARTIST: Jack Straka
TITLE: Untitled bowl
MATERIALS: Koa
DIMENSIONS: 7"H x 7"Dia

THE PURIST AESTHETIC

A Perfect Form in Beautiful Wood

One does not need to be an art critic to appreciate the intrinsic beauty of a richly figured wood and the calm, gentle lines of a finely crafted vessel. The wood offers a manuscript of its life, echoing its joys and hardships with every grain, and drawing one in. Wood is a living material, and we can relate to its struggles; in a way it seems to mirror our lives. To a large extent it is the richness of the wood that has rocketed this relatively new medium to stardom.

It is difficult to imagine a better object than the vessel to present the incomparable beauty of wood. It is a canvas uniquely suited to take advantage of the wood's inherent organic traits. A natural edge may evolve up from the base of a classical form. Bark inclusions, insect damage and spalting can be revealed on the open surface of an unadorned bowl.

As a counterpoint to the beauty of the wood, a graceful and elegant form can transcend the material from which it is made and speak directly to our sense of balance and design. We respond universally to the curves, angles, and clean smooth lines of a timeless form.

The founding artists in turned wood began the exploration of work celebrating the perfect union of wood and form. Marked by simplicity and clarity, this purist aesthetic is as valid today as thirty years ago. In a field which is producing sculpture and work of ever greater complexity, it is refreshing and rejuvenating to experience this marriage of material and shape, where the artist's responsibility is to find the most direct way of exposing and presenting nature's beauty.

TWO

Liam O'Neill

ARTIST: Liam O'Neill
TITLE: Untitled vessel
MATERIALS: Spalted beech
DIMENSIONS: 6"H x 9"Dia

John Jordan

Photo: George Chambers

ARTIST: John Jordan
TITLE: Untitled vase form
MATERIALS: Maple
DIMENSIONS: 7"H x 8"Dia

John Dodge Meyer

ARTIST: John Dodge Meyer
TITLE: Tornado Logic
MATERIALS: Spalted sugarberry
DIMENSIONS: 5^1/$_2$"H x 8^1/$_2$"W x 8"D

The irony of the title of the *Tornado Logic Series* is that such storms are neither logical nor predictable. Neither is the abstraction of design caused by the fungal spalting that quickly took over this storm-mangled tree. The work proves the axiom that what is chaotic and terrifying in life can become exhilarating and enthralling in art.

Photo: Rob Jaffe

ARTIST: Christian Burchard
TITLE: Vessels
MATERIALS: Blackwood
DIMENSIONS: 3"H x 3"Dia to 6"H x 6"Dia

Dan Kvitka

ARTIST: Dan Kvitka
TITLE: Untitled vessel
MATERIALS: Macassar ebony
DIMENSIONS: 9"H x 12¹/₂"Dia

"The significance of the vessel, both
functional and decorative, has for millennia
attached us to who we are and where
we have come from," says Dan Kvitka.
"Creating vessels in wood gives me a
sense of place within this history, and I find
this exploration exceptionally exciting."

Photo: Paul G. Beswick

ARTIST: Ed Moulthrop
TITLE: Ellipsoid
MATERIALS: Leopard maple (acer rubrum)
DIMENSIONS: 8"H x 20"Dia

Bob Stocksdale

ARTIST: Bob Stocksdale
TITLE: Untitled bowl
MATERIALS: Pacific yew
DIMENSIONS: 3¼"H x 4¾"Dia

ARTIST: Bruce Mitchell
TITLE: Bizenta
MATERIALS: Redwood burl
DIMENSIONS: 8³/₄"H x 8¹/₂"W x 7"D

Ron Kent

Photo: Rae Huo

ARTIST: Ron Kent
TITLE: Untitled bowl
MATERIALS: Norfolk Island pine
DIMENSIONS: 11"H x 11"Dia

Photo: Tony Boase

ARTIST: Ray Key
TITLE: Footed flange bowl
MATERIALS: Pink ivory wood
DIMENSIONS: 3$\frac{1}{2}$"H x 6$\frac{1}{2}$"Dia

Pink ivory is the rarest wood in the world. It grows in remote areas of South Africa, and for centuries it has been a sacred wood to the Zulu people. By tradition, only a chief can fell a tree. Others possessing this wood may be killed. This piece takes on a sacred nature in both its form and the wood used.

Photo: Tony Boase

ARTIST: Ray Key
TITLE: Footed incurved bowl
MATERIALS: Burr buckeye
DIMENSIONS: 4$\frac{1}{2}$"H x 8"Dia

John Dodge Meyer

ARTIST: John Dodge Meyer

TITLE: Vase form

MATERIALS: Blackheart persimmon

DIMENSIONS: 6³/₄"H x 8¹/₂"W x 8⁷/₈"D

"We call the destruction of replaceable man-made items *vandalism,* while the destruction of irreplaceable natural resources is called *development,*" comments John Dodge Meyer. Meyer works with non-endangered North American hardwoods which have been victims of storms, development, disease or age. "With these lathe-turned forms, I seek to assist the viewer and collector toward an aesthetic temperament based on nature, dignity and timeless beauty. Nothing less than the planet is at stake."

Mark Lindquist

ARTIST: Mark Lindquist
TITLE: Turned bowl
MATERIALS: Spalted yellow birch burl
DIMENSIONS: 9"H x 15 1/2"Dia
COLLECTION: The Art Institute of
Chicago (Gift of Arthur and Jane Mason)

Bert Marsh

ARTIST: Bert Marsh
TITLE: Natural edge bowl
MATERIALS: Burr maple
DIMENSIONS: 5"H x 8"Dia

Photo: Tony Boase

ARTIST: Bert Marsh
TITLE: Untitled bowl
MATERIALS: Spalted elm
DIMENSIONS: 5"H x 8"Dia

Photo: Tony Boase

Christian Burchard

Photo: Rob Jaffe

ARTIST: Christian Burchard
TITLE: Basket forms
MATERIALS: Madrone burl
DIMENSIONS: $1/2$"H x $1/2$"Dia
to 8"H x 8"Dia

The wood in these basket forms of
madrone burl warps as it dries, creating
works with distinct character.

ARTIST: Ron Fleming
TITLE: Datura
MATERIALS: Basswood and acrylic
DIMENSIONS: 13½" X 17"Dia

THE VESSEL TRANSFORMED

Carving and Surface Treatments

Contemporary craft has long struggled to prove that function, or history of function, does not exempt it from being art. Woodturners present us with work that forces a reconsideration of craft as art: the vessel that does not hold water, or the bowl obviously never intended for use. These artists speak the language of craft, where the vessel is a vessel in the sense that we are all vessels. As we might be said to contain spirit, vessels suggest that they, too, represent this particular sense of containment. It is an analogy which has existed since ancient times, and runs through primitive as well as contemporary work.

Art is not about response to an inanimate object, but rather a relationship between people: the artist and the viewer. A painting is seen not as an object, but as an extension of the artist — and the viewer is part of a dialog. When it comes to the medium of wood, the voice of nature is included, and the dialog becomes a conversation between nature, artist and viewer.

To open the discussion, woodturners have chosen a variety of methods to make the vessel speak for them. From simple texturing to the most detailed carving, manipulating the surface of a piece allows the artist to add another level of communication in concert with, or in counterpoint to, the vessel form. Sandblasting, bleaching, burning and painting change the perception — and thereby the story being told. Piercing, inlaying or combining materials add pattern and contrast to play against the grain of a solid piece of wood. Carving, whether highly representational imagery or bold abstract expression, can change the silhouette of a piece without changing its intrinsic form.

Each of these approaches is merely a means to an end. The variety and complexity of these techniques attest to the vitality of the field and its potential for growth. The vessel: transformed into art.

THREE

J. Paul Fennell

ARTIST: J. Paul Fennell
TITLE: Untitled vessel
MATERIALS: African sumac
DIMENSIONS: 9"H x 6½"Dia

Photos: Dana Davis

ARTIST: Gene Pozzesi
TITLE: Untitled platter form
MATERIALS: Jarrah burl
DIMENSIONS: 2¾"H x 17"Dia

The artist employed a unique technique of
burning the wood to create the texture
around the rim of this platter form.

Michael Peterson

Photos: Roger Schreiber

ARTIST: Michael Peterson
TITLE: Canyon Wind
MATERIALS: Redwood burl
DIMENSIONS: 8"H x 12"Dia

The artist has carved and sandblasted this
piece to suggest a wind-worn landscape.

Michelle Holzapfel

Photos: David Holzapfel

ARTIST: Michelle Holzapfel
TITLE: Linked vessels
MATERIALS: Spalted sugar maple
DIMENSIONS: Vase: 14"H x 7"Dia, bowl: 7"W x 13"L

These two permanently linked vessels were turned
and carved from a single piece of wood. Pyrography
(literally, writing with fire) was used to create drama.

Giles Gilson

ARTIST: Giles Gilson
TITLE: Big Window/Little Bowl
MATERIALS: Walnut, maple and lacquers
DIMENSIONS: 3¹/₂"H x 5"Dia

ARTIST: Gael Montgomerie
TITLE: Untitled vessel
MATERIALS: Painted sycamore
DIMENSIONS: 5"H x 9¹/₂"Dia

"Because I believe that woodworkers must help direct demand away from beautiful but increasingly rare timbers, I do most of my turning in sycamore," explains New Zealand artist Gael Montgomerie. "Sycamore's silvery paleness makes it an ideal vehicle for my exploration of surface decoration through carving, coloring and calligraphy. I use artists' acrylic paint because I like to work fast and I can get a range from subtle wash to vibrant hues, yet the wood still shows through."

David Groth

ARTIST: David Groth
TITLE: Terrifying Fish
MATERIALS: Myrtlewood
DIMENSIONS: 10"H x 12"W x 11"D

Ron Fleming

ARTIST: Ron Fleming
TITLE: New Beginnings
MATERIALS: Redwood burl
DIMENSIONS: 13"H x 19"Dia

Stephen Hogbin

ARTIST: Stephen Hogbin
TITLE: Breaking Wave Bowl
MATERIALS: Beech and acrylic paint
DIMENSIONS: 5"H x 9"Dia

The artist's interest in ritual objects
and their functional necessity led him to
experiment with cutting and reassembling
turned wood forms to create objects
which ritualized everyday activities.

Hans Weissflog

ARTIST: Hans Weissflog
TITLE: Rocking Bowl
MATERIALS: Bocote
DIMENSIONS: 4"H x 6¹/₂"Dia

Frank Sudol

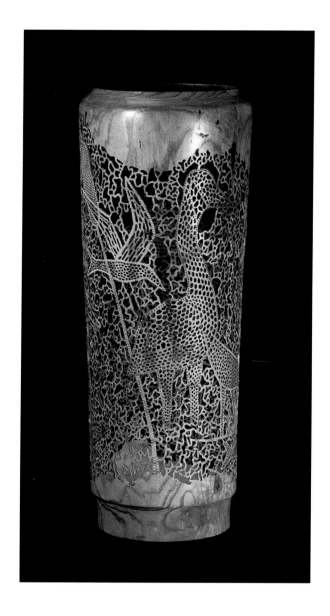

ARTIST: Frank Sudol

TITLE: A View of the Swamp

MATERIALS: Ash, acrylic and lacquer

DIMENSIONS: 25"H x 9"Dia

The wall thickness of this delicate vessel is $\frac{1}{16}$th of an inch. It has been meticulously carved by high-speed drills.

Terry Martin

ARTIST: Terry Martin
TITLE: Huon Dream #1
MATERIALS: Huon pine
DIMENSIONS: 4¹/₂"H x 9"Dia

Melvyn Firmager

ARTIST: Melvyn Firmager
TITLE: Seaflower Vessel
MATERIALS: Eucalyptus
DIMENSIONS: 4³/₄"H x 5"W x 4"D

Stephen Hughes

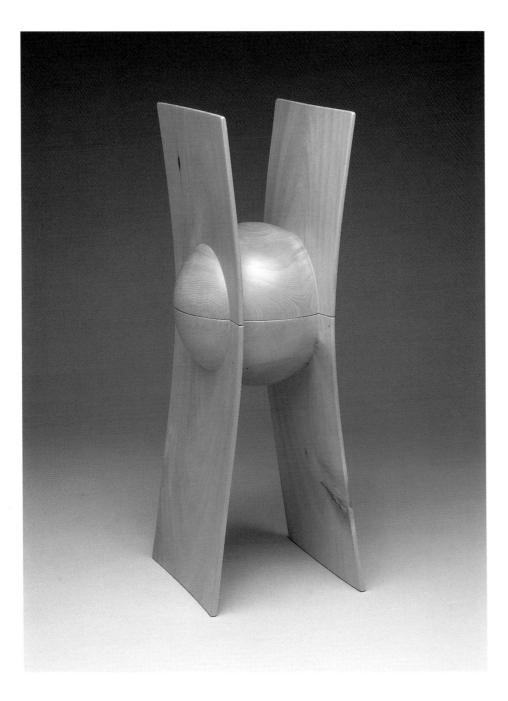

ARTIST: Stephen Hughes
TITLE: Vader Box
MATERIALS: Boxwood
DIMENSIONS: 16"H x 5"W x 4"Dia

Hayley Smith

ARTIST: Hayley Smith
TITLE: Hemispherical Bowl
MATERIALS: English sycamore
DIMENSIONS: 3$^1/_2$"H x 8$^1/_2$"Dia

Clay Foster

ARTIST: Clay Foster
TITLE: Serpentine Talk
MATERIALS: Oak, galvanized sheet iron,
brass brads, eggshell and paint
DIMENSIONS: 16"H x 6"Dia

John Jordan

ARTIST: John Jordan
TITLE: Untitled vase
MATERIALS: Cherry
DIMENSIONS: 5"H x 6"Dia

The artist uses carving techniques to alter and accentuate form, as well as to create texture. Most of the woods he uses come from the dump, construction sites and the like. "I find great satisfaction in creating objects from material that was destined to be buried or burned," he explains.

Michael Hosaluk

Photo: Grant Kernan

ARTIST: Michael Hosaluk
TITLE: Future Species
MATERIALS: Elm, amber and paint
DIMENSIONS: 13"H x 4"Dia

David Sengel

Photos: George Chambers

ARTIST: David Sengel
TITLE: Fish Bowl
MATERIALS: Western cedar, box elder,
rose and locust thorns
DIMENSIONS: 15$\frac{1}{2}$"H x 7"Dia

This piece is both whimsical and suggestive
of a ceremonial urn. It features the artist's
trademark use of thorns as a textural and
expressive element.

Michelle Holzapfel

Photos: David Holzapfel

ARTIST: Michelle Holzapfel
TITLE: Serpent Bowl
MATERIALS: Cherry burl
DIMENSIONS: 5"H x 16"Dia

A carved snake creates a sense of the mythological in this bowl form, which features pyrography.

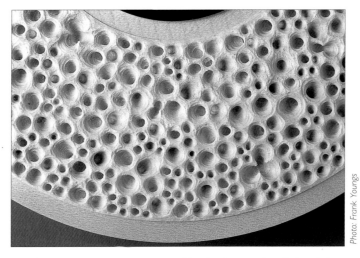

Photo: Frank Youngs

ARTIST: Hayley Smith
TITLE: Untitled platter (detail)
MATERIALS: English sycamore
DIMENSIONS: 1¼"H x 10¼"Dia

The contemporary forms of Hayley Smith are about balance, form and material, and feature a unique approach to surface texture. Her experience in two-dimensional disciplines such as etching and printmaking are expanded upon in three-dimensional wood forms.

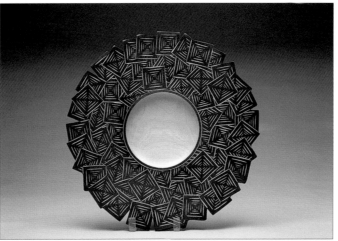

ARTIST: Al Stirt
TITLE: Crowded Square Bowl
MATERIALS: Painted maple
DIMENSIONS: 15"Dia x 3"D

Al Stirt seeks to transcend the decorative, believing that a craft object created with skill, dedication and care says something about the maker. "The greatest joy for me is finding a personal and unique form of expression utilizing forms that have been used for at least ten thousand years," he explains.

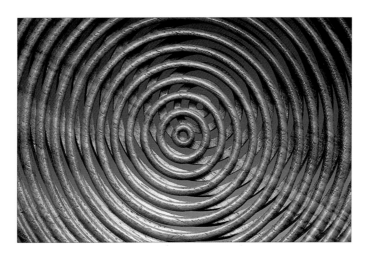

ARTIST: Hans Weissflog
TITLE: Spider Bowl (detail)
MATERIALS: Mambode
DIMENSIONS: 3"H x 8"Dia

Turned and cut through on either side, Hans Weissflog's bowls create interesting optical effects such as the Moiré pattern on the interior of this Spider Bowl.

Mike Scott

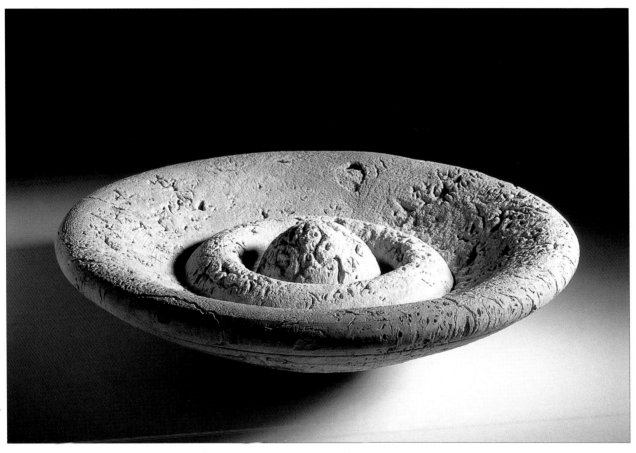

Photo: Tony Boase

ARTIST: Mike Scott
TITLE: Tumulus
MATERIALS: Oak burl
DIMENSIONS: $3\frac{1}{2}$"H x 13"Dia

Michael Lee

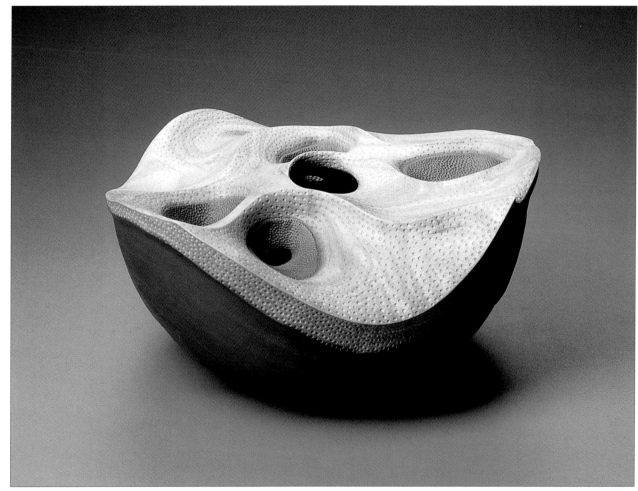

Photo: Hugo De Vries

ARTIST: Michael Lee
TITLE: Tidal Pod
MATERIALS: Milo
DIMENSIONS: 5¹/₂"H x 10¹/₂"Dia

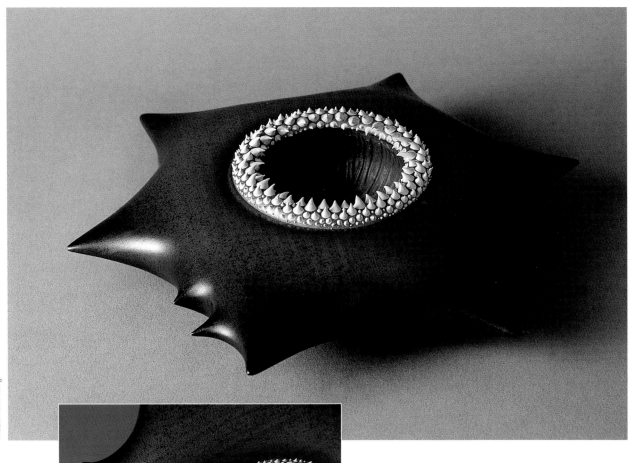

Photos: Frank Youngs

ARTIST: Louise Hibbert
TITLE: Radiolarian Vessel III
MATERIALS: English sycamore, polyester
resin, acrylic ink and acrylic texture paste
DIMENSIONS: 25"Dia

"Inspiration for my work comes from
a wide range of visual sources. Simple
organisms — sea life, insects, fossilized
creatures — offer a wealth of intriguing
forms, textures and color combinations.
I carve the wood after turning, and use
paint, colored waxes, scorching, resin and
metal to create the effects that I require."

ARTIST: Robert J. Cutler

TITLE: Good Times

MATERIALS: Birch, eucalyptus, sterling
silver, brass, fossilized bone and antler

DIMENSIONS: 6"H x 11"Dia

THE CONSTRUCTED VESSEL

Rather than starting and ending with a single piece of wood that can dictate form and design, the constructed vessel reflects the total intention of the artist. By definition, it is created from the assemblage of parts. This allows for endless combinations utilizing the vast assortment of colors and grain patterns that wood has to offer.

Contemporary wood artists have developed and perfected ways of creating ever more complex constructions; stacked lamination, segmentation and joinery are all used to achieve spectacular results. Stacked lamination is achieved by gluing up multiple layers of wood, one on top of the other. As the pieces are turned or carved to reveal the layers, the pattern emerges. In some cases, the artist chooses to further manipulate the surface with pigmentation, adding another dimension to the finished piece.

Segmentation involves multiple pieces of wood that are glued together in a predetermined pattern and then turned to their final form. Masters of this technique often utilize thousands of individual pieces of wood in a single finished vessel. The individual segments may vary in size, as determined by the design function of that particular element. This work is probably the most demanding and time consuming of all techniques used in contemporary woodturning. Each cut must be precise so that seams become almost invisible. The placement of each segment must be mathematically calculated to ensure the desired design.

Constructed vessels also include those in which elements have been turned or carved, then joined to produce the final composition. This technique is most often used in sculptural work, with striking effect. No matter which technique has been chosen, constructed turned wood delivers the message of the artist with remarkable clarity and ingenuity.

FOUR

Gary Johnson

ARTIST: Gary Johnson
TITLE: Untitled vessel
MATERIALS: Tulipwood and bloodwood
DIMENSIONS: 10"H x 6"Dia

Gianfranco Angelino

ARTIST: Gianfranco Angelino
TITLE: Multi-Layered Platter
MATERIALS: Various woods
DIMENSIONS: 3"H x 14"Dia

"It is a privilege of woodturners to use materials obtained from a large variety of trees, to be able to employ of each tree the widest description of parts and to bring out the aesthetic value of timber which is considered unsuitable for general use."

Mike Shuler

ARTIST: Mike Shuler
TITLE: Untitled bowl
MATERIALS: Brazilian tulipwood
DIMENSIONS: 2³/₄"H x 5"Dia

Photos: Tim Barnwell

ARTIST: Ray Jones
TITLE: Untitled box
MATERIALS: Laminated baltic birch,
madrone burl and ebony
DIMENSIONS: 5"H x 11"Dia

This functional jewelry box features
a hinged door and a rotating tray.

Rude Osolnik

ARTIST: Rude Osolnik
TITLE: Untitled vessel
MATERIALS: Laminated birch
DIMENSIONS: 9$^1/_2$"H x 9$^1/_2$"D

Osolnik has been recognized by
the Museum of Science and Industry
for his creative use of waste products
in the wood industry.

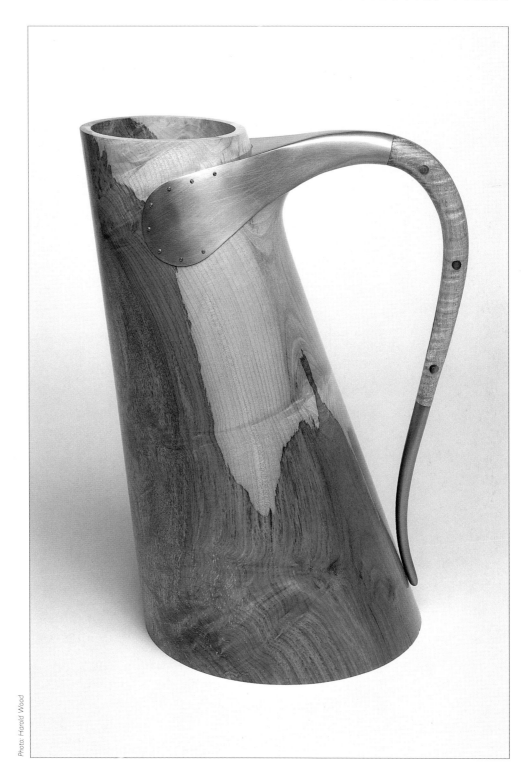

Photo: Harold Wood

William Moore

ARTIST: William Moore
TITLE: Aragon
MATERIALS: Myrtle and bronze
DIMENSIONS: 20"H x 17"W x 12"D

This is one of many works in which William Moore explores pitcher and bucket forms. "In this series, I have shifted the axis to a diagonal to create a more dynamic sense of movement. Also important is the relationship of the handle to the body of the object. In *Aragon,* the body is a truncated cone form, with strong straight edges to its shape. Relating the bold tapering curve of the handle to this shape enhances its gestural movement and adds energy to the total composition."

Philip Moulthrop

Photo: Paul Beswick

ARTIST: Philip Moulthrop
TITLE: Mosaic bowl
MATERIALS: White pine
DIMENSIONS: 12"H x 20"Dia

Photo: Paul Beswick

ARTIST: Philip Moulthrop
TITLE: Bundled Form Mosaic Bowls
MATERIALS: White pine and cherry
DIMENSIONS: 9"H x 10"Dia,
7"H x 8¼"Dia, 6"H x 6¼"Dia

Robert J. Cutler

ARTIST: Robert J. Cutler
TITLE: Exaltation
MATERIALS: Diamond willow, birch, walnut, silver, brass, fossilized bone and antler
DIMENSIONS: 4"H x 19"Dia

Robert Cutler creates turned, lidded vessels with intricate inlays of various woods from around the world, precious and semi-precious metals, fossils and prehistoric materials found primarily in Alaska, where he lives. The pieces are finished with his own formula that seals and protects, while enhancing the three-dimensional properties of the wood.

Gianfranco Angelino

ARTIST: Gianfranco Angelino
TITLE: Multi-Layered Platter
MATERIALS: Birch, mahogany and plywood
DIMENSIONS: 3"H x 14"Dia

Many of the most charming woods are of small dimensions, and irregular. Gianfranco Angelino has spent years developing new techniques and tools to make the exploitation of special portions of branches, roots, knots, bifurcates, and the stalks of small shrubs technically feasible.

Ray Allen

ARTIST: Ray Allen
TITLE: Seed Bowl #8
MATERIALS: Purpleheart, ebony, maple
and tagua nut
DIMENSIONS: 5$\frac{1}{2}$"H x 5$\frac{1}{4}$"Dia

ARTIST: Ray Allen

TITLE: Untitled vessel

MATERIALS: Zebrawood, wenge and ziricote

DIMENSIONS: 6½"H x 9½"Dia

"I am inspired by Southwest and prehistoric pottery. The challenge of constructing intricate designs gives me the challenge I need. The finished piece gives me the self-satisfaction I enjoy."

Giles Gilson

Photo: Rick Siciliano

ARTIST: Giles Gilson
TITLE: Interpretation III
MATERIALS: Various exotic and
domestic woods
DIMENSIONS: 6"H x 8"Dia

This 1981 piece is an early example of
a segmented turned wood bowl with the
inclusion of narrative aspects in the work.

ARTIST: Bud Latven
TITLE: Maple Bowl, Segmented Bowl Series
MATERIALS: Fiddleback maple, African
ebony and veneers
DIMENSIONS: 5"H x 9"Dia

Jean-François Escoulen

ARTIST: Jean-François Escoulen
TITLE: La Cruche en Folie
(The Crazy Pitcher)
MATERIALS: Turned and carved sycamore,
cocobolo and pernambucco
DIMENSIONS: 10½" x 13" x 9"

ARTIST: Paul Fletcher
TITLE: Centerpiece
MATERIALS: African blackwood,
alternative ivory, boxwood, cocus
wood and dymondwood
DIMENSIONS: 13¼"H x 6⅝"Dia

A masterpiece of ornamental turning,
this constructed form features a great deal
of inlay work and ornamental detail work.
"I am privileged to work on the last true
Rose Engine lathe built by Holtzapffel,
the Stradivarius of lathe makers, over 150
years ago," says Fletcher, who has won
every prize offered by the Society of
Ornamental Turners and the Worshipful
Company of Turners in his native England.
"I am constantly challenged by the
patience, techniques and curious spatial
awareness that are needed to explore
the infinite potential of so rare a tool."

Michael Mode

Photos: Alex Williams

ARTIST: Michael Mode
TITLE: Akbar's Affinity
MATERIALS: Holly, ebony, purpleheart, pink ivory and wenge
DIMENSIONS: 12"H x 19½"W x 12"D

"My motivation comes from an intense life-long inspiration to create and bring into existence the objects of my imagination. These have included, over the years, poetry, painting, drawing, music and, finally, turned wood vessels and objects. The character and style of my work reflects my fascination with the art and architecture of northern India and the Middle East."

ARTIST: Stephen Paulsen
TITLE: Untitled perfume bottle
MATERIALS: Various woods
DIMENSIONS: 7"H x 2½"W x ½"D

ARTIST: Jack Slentz
TITLE: A Group of Friends
MATERIALS: Various woods
DIMENSIONS: from 19"H x 5"Dia
to 25¹/₂"H x 6"Dia

WOODTURNING AS SCULPTURE

The medium of wood is certainly not new to contemporary art. Constantin Brancusi crafted many of his important sculptures in wood. Henry Moore, Hans Arp and Isamu Noguchi are just three of the artists who have been intrigued by the possibilities of the medium. For the most part, these well-known artists used traditional carving techniques to shape their forms. Today, a new breed of artist has discovered the diverse possibilities of working with the lathe.

Sculptural work in the field of woodturning is a relatively new phenomenon. Traditionally, the lathe has been associated with functional objects. Once considered a trade tool, it has become central to the creation of contemporary wood art. New attachments and techniques allow the artist to do things on the lathe that had previously been impossible. One of the most innovative advancements in the field is multi-axis turning. This technique, in which the artist places the wood onto the lathe in multiple positions, creates designs that are truly unique, and has allowed many "wood artists" to find a niche for themselves in the broader art world. Artists are also using the lathe as a tool to rough out an initial sculptural form before applying any of a myriad of other treatments. Turning — in combination with hand carving, sandblasting, texturing, painting or assemblage — results in a fresh new approach to the sculptural form.

Unlike traditional art sculpture, work being created in the field of turned wood does not have a strong tradition to fall back on. Artists working in craft media usually come from a background of function, and their influences are derived from other media as well as the natural world. Sculptural work in woodturning began with the large-scale vessel and has evolved to a place where the wood has become secondary to the design of the piece, and the medium is not always immediately recognizable. As new techniques are generated and the artists' experience matures, sculptural woodturning will continue to develop into an even more exciting art medium.

FIVE

Mark Lindquist

ARTIST: Mark Lindquist
TITLE: Prisoner #1A
MATERIALS: Lignum vitae
DIMENSIONS: 9"H x 7"W x 8"D

Photo: Paul Avis

Stoney Lamar

Photo: Tim Barnwell

ARTIST: Stoney Lamar
TITLE: Muse
MATERIALS: Madrone
DIMENSIONS: 15"H x 13"W x 12"D

"The work begins as a relationship I have established with a particular piece of wood and reflects how its characteristics will interplay with my intentions and my emerging techniques and conceptual vocabulary. As I adjust the work's axis and continue turning, new challenges and possibilities are constantly presented, thereby allowing a subtractive process to become an intriguing way of constructing an object. The resulting figurative, architectural or abstract object is an attempt to create balance and tension by juxtaposing asymmetrical and symmetrical elements."

Robyn Horn

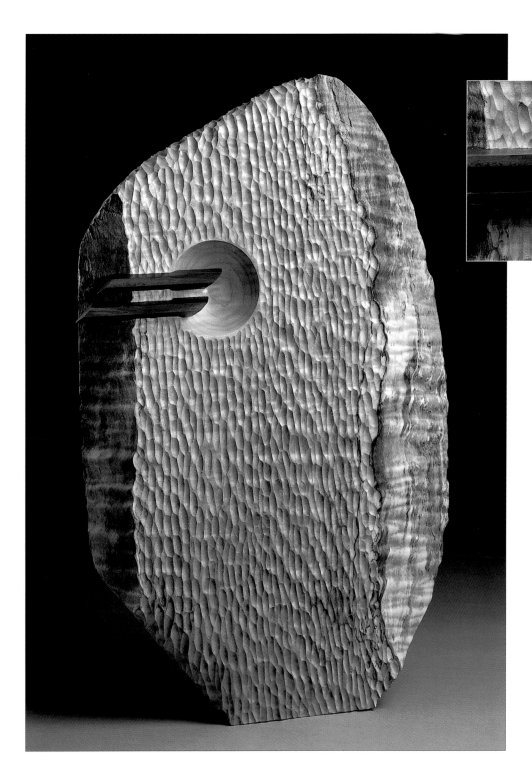

Photos: George Chambers

ARTIST: Robyn Horn
TITLE: Standing Stone
MATERIALS: Fiddleback maple,
Macassar ebony
DIMENSIONS: 24"H x 15"W x 2½"D

Todd Hoyer

ARTIST: Todd Hoyer
TITLE: Disc Series
MATERIALS: Sycamore and wire
DIMENSIONS: 18¼"H x 21"W x 5"D

"This piece reveals forms within forms, layers
upon layers, a theme that runs through my work
and my life."

Mark Sfirri

ARTIST: Mark Sfirri
TITLE: Candlesticks
MATERIALS: Cherry
DIMENSIONS: 9"H to 13"H

Photos: Tim Barnwell

ARTIST: Stoney Lamar
TITLE: No Looking Back
MATERIALS: Bleached madrone
DIMENSIONS: 20"H x 10"W x 5"D

"The development and use of multiple-axis turning techniques as a way of applying texture or sculpting asymmetrical forms on the lathe has allowed me to transcend the round object and to create a sense of image and movement that is suggestive of what I see while the object is being formed on the lathe. A multiple-axis approach has also allowed me to draw from a wider range of influences and to develop a more personal imagery and narrative."

William Hunter

Photo: Hap Sakwa

ARTIST: William Hunter

TITLE: Tangled

MATERIALS: Cocobolo

DIMENSIONS: 6"H x 14"W x 14"D

The relationship between these two sculptural forms provides a sense of both tension and intimacy. The two forms can be combined in a variety of ways to create varying sculptural statements.

Photo: Randy Johnson

ARTIST: Betty Scarpino
TITLE: She Moves On
(Missing Piece Series)
MATERIALS: Maple
DIMENSIONS: 1½"H x 8"Dia

Connie Mississippi

ARTIST: Connie Mississippi
TITLE: Egg
MATERIALS: Laminated oak dowels
DIMENSIONS: 6"H x 9"W x 6"D

Rolly Munro

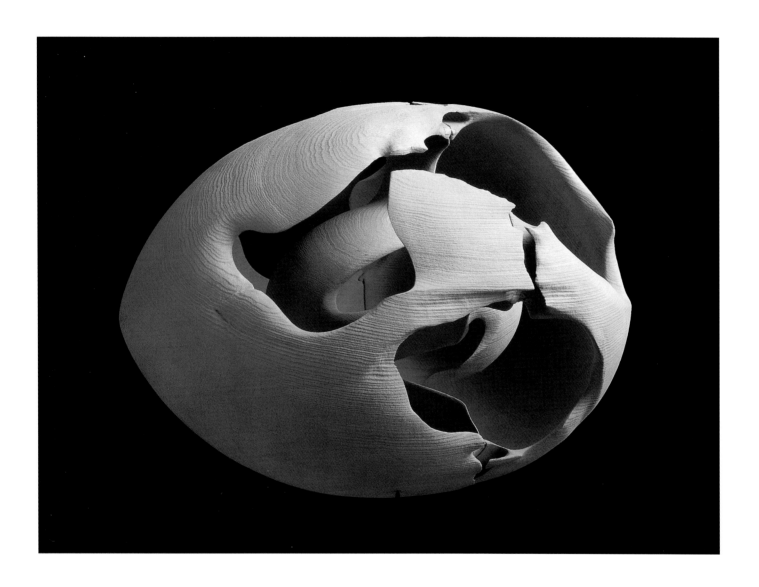

ARTIST: Rolly Munro
TITLE: Flotsam
MATERIALS: Kauri
DIMENSIONS: 12"H x 15"W x 15"D

This piece has been turned, carved and sandblasted. Its form is derived from weathered, washed-up shell, bone and driftwood found in abundance on the southern shores of New Zealand.

Merryll Saylan

ARTIST: Merryll Saylan
TITLE: The Breakfast Tray
MATERIALS: Maple
DIMENSIONS: 5"H x 23½"W x 17"D

From the artist's series of sculptural
"still lifes."

Ben Trupperbäumer

ARTIST: Ben Trupperbäumer
TITLE: Muricidae
MATERIALS: Acacia
DIMENSIONS: 20"H x 27¹/₂"W x 3"D

Virginia Dotson

ARTIST: Virginia Dotson
TITLE: Silver Lining #12
MATERIALS: Pau marfim plywood,
dye and paint
DIMENSIONS: 12"H x 8¹/₄"Dia

The spiral path leading from the base
to the top of the vessel reveals views
of the interior which change with the
viewing angle. Where it is seen through
the cuts in the vessel wall, the dark
metallic interior surface contrasts with
the matte black exterior.

Steve Loar • Mark Sfirri

Photos: N. Stuart

ARTISTS: Steve Loar and Mark Sfirri
TITLE: Nikki's Lurid Past Comes Calling
MATERIALS: Poplar, cherry burl and mixed media
DIMENSIONS: 28"H x 10"W x 12"D

Working with a rough figure by Mark Sfirri, Steve Loar created a work inspired by a character in the novel *The Collector Collector*. It explores the guarded reality of one's past contrasted with what is projected to the world.

William Moore

ARTIST: William Moore
TITLE: In the Balance
MATERIALS: Koa, bronze and limestone
DIMENSIONS: 9$\frac{1}{2}$"H x 17$\frac{3}{4}$"W x 3$\frac{3}{4}$"D

Photo: George Chambers

ARTIST: Robyn Horn
TITLE: Slashed Millstone
MATERIALS: Ebonized redwood burl
DIMENSIONS: 22"H x 20"W x 8"D

"With my *Millstone Series*, there is such a strong implication of the old world in the form, the feeling of hard work, and the struggle to survive. With endless combinations of furrow patterns and texture decoration, they have a structural strength and a symmetrical balance."

Hugh McKay

ARTIST: Hugh McKay
TITLE: Tripot #5
MATERIALS: Maple burl
DIMENSIONS: 11"H x 11"W x 9"D

ARTIST: David Sengel
TITLE: Zen Moon
MATERIALS: Maple burl, laurel root and hercules club thorns
DIMENSIONS: 16½"H x 17"W x 8"D

David Sengel took a circuitous route to a life of turning wood. The artist gained an appreciation of wood at an early age in his father's amateur woodworking shop. After studying music at Davidson College in North Carolina, he opened his own business repairing and restoring pianos. Concurrently, he began to work more with wood and purchased a lathe out of a catalog. Largely self-taught, Sengel also took classes at Arrowmont School (instructors included Del Stubbs and David Ellsworth), which gave him the technical skills and desire to pursue lathe-oriented woodworking full-time. He has been making his living as a full-time woodturner since 1987.

Dennis Elliott

ARTIST: Dennis Elliott
TITLE: Ursa Major
MATERIALS: Big leaf maple burl
DIMENSIONS: 40"H x 43"W x 3"D

Stephen Hughes • Margaret Salt

ARTISTS: Stephen Hughes and Margaret Salt
TITLE: Eruption #2
MATERIALS: Jarrah burl, acrylic
paint and gold leaf
DIMENSIONS: 47"Dia x 4¹/₄"D

Rude Osolnik

ARTIST: Rude Osolnik
TITLE: Untitled vessel
MATERIALS: Distressed maple burl
DIMENSIONS: 6"H x 11"D

Natural edges and insect damage give this piece
a striking, worn appearance.

Jack Straka

ARTIST: Jack Straka
TITLE: Untitled sculpture
MATERIALS: Mango with ebony base
DIMENSIONS: 16"H x 6"Dia

Often a sculptural form is the best way
of capturing the natural beauty of a piece
of wood. Such is the case with this piece
by master woodturner Jack Straka.

Mike Scott

Photo: Tony Boase

ARTIST: Mike Scott
TITLE: Fluted form
MATERIALS: Oak burl
DIMENSIONS: 8"H x 8"Dia

The artist works primarily in local woods,
such as elm and oak, which are in a state
of degradation. He finds the inspiration in
the piece of wood, rather than a precon-
ceived idea. This form has been turned,
sandblasted and bleached.

David Ellsworth

ARTIST: David Ellsworth
TITLE: Kata-Kamal
MATERIALS: Ash
(burned and burnished)
DIMENSIONS: 11"H x 11"Dia
and 15"H x 15"Dia

ARTIST: Todd Hoyer
TITLE: Untitled bowl
MATERIALS: Scorched box elder with grout
DIMENSIONS: 2³/₈"H x 5¹/₄"Dia

S M A L L   T R E A S U R E S

L iving in a bigger-is-better, dollar-per-inch world, it takes increased sensitivity to appreciate the importance of small objects. If a painting or sculpture is an extension of the artist, and the work is "larger than life," then one can easily assume that it is the work of a "big artist." It is refreshing, then, to discover that this is not necessarily true. The small turned wood object has an added power due to its size, and can be appreciated with a rare intimacy unique to work in this scale.

There has been a growing interest in small wood objects, pieces which are precious and are best suited to being observed in detail. The beauty is not limited to the visual, however; these objects are tactile and inspire one to touch them. From the hand of the artist to the hand of the beholder, this is one of the pleasures of wood brought to its fullest accessibility. One relates differently to a small wood piece; holding it in the hand as something dear, one experiences it in a manner distinct from other art forms.

Describing his **Spirit Form** series, master turner David Ellsworth notes that small-scale pieces can have "a certain power that has less to do with their actual size than how we humans perceive them in relationship to ourselves. While a large object viewed at a great distance might appear the same in scale as a small object viewed up close, it is the small object that captures the focus of our personal energy."

Many woodturners work in small scale on occasion, in much the same way that a painter might create sketches or a sculptor maquettes. There are also those who concentrate their efforts on small dimensions, often developing techniques and tools especially suited to their needs. In either case, a small form cannot lean on presence or power in the same way that a large work can, and any failure in the form becomes obvious. The following pages present a number of approaches to small scale; you are certain to agree that all are treasures.

S I X

Stephen Hughes

ARTIST: Stephen Hughes
TITLE: Enchanted Vessel
MATERIALS: Red gum, huon
pine and beefwood
DIMENSIONS: 2^1/$_2$"H x 4^3/$_4$"W x 2^1/$_4$"D

Gary Sanders

ARTIST: Gary Sanders
TITLE: Space Station
MATERIALS: Tulipwood and box elder burl
DIMENSIONS: 2"H x 6½"W x 3"D

David Ellsworth

ARTIST: David Ellsworth
TITLE: Spirit Form
MATERIALS: Black ash burl
DIMENSIONS: 2"H x 2³/₄"Dia

David Sengel

ARTIST: David Sengel
TITLE: Lidded container
MATERIALS: Buckeye burl and rose thorns
DIMENSIONS: 1³/₄"H x 3¹/₄"Dia

The addition of thorns to this container form
creates a sense of protection and mystery.

Kip Christensen

ARTIST: Kip Christensen
TITLE: Lidded container
MATERIALS: Pink ivory, ebony, bone,
moose antler
DIMENSIONS: 3$\frac{1}{2}$"H x 2"Dia

Photos: Dan Haab

Craig Lossing

ARTIST: Craig Lossing
TITLE: Untitled lidded container
MATERIALS: Bocote and ebony
DIMENSIONS: 4"H x 3"Dia

"In my current work creating small
containers with ornate lids, I use classical
forms for the bases," says Lossing.
"There is a certain comfort in these forms
because they have always been with us,
and I focus on discovering the unseen in
what has already been seen." The covers
are created to add contrast and be kinetic,
to give motion and energy to what is
serene and stable.

Jon Sauer

Photo: Richard Sargent

ARTIST: Jon Sauer
TITLE: Carved box
MATERIALS: African blackwood
(pink ivory wood inside)
DIMENSIONS: 3"H x 3"Dia

Jon Sauer

Photo: Richard Sargent

ARTIST: Jon Sauer
TITLE: Perfume bottle
MATERIALS: African blackwood and
bloodwood
DIMENSIONS: 5"H x 1½"Dia

Jon Sauer employs an antique ornamental
lathe made in 1868 by the Holtzapffel
family to create his perfume bottles and
boxes. The ornamentation in his turnings
is done manually by indexing the work and
carving it with a small revolving cutter.

Andrew Potocnik

Andrew Potocnik

ARTIST: Andrew Potocnik
TITLE: Lidded containers
MATERIALS: Red gum and paint
DIMENSIONS: 1³/₄"H x 3¹/₂"Dia

Johannes Michelsen

ARTIST: Johannes Michelsen
TITLE: Miniature Hat Rack with Four Hats
MATERIALS: Various woods
DIMENSIONS: 6"H x 2½"W x 2½"D

Vic Wood

ARTIST: Vic Wood
TITLE: Untitled container
MATERIALS: Sheoak
DIMENSIONS: 3"H x 8"W x 6"D

Richard Raffan

ARTIST: Richard Raffan
TITLE: Untitled bowl
MATERIALS: Jarrah
DIMENSIONS: 1¹/₂"H x 6"Dia

Bob Stocksdale

ARTIST: Bob Stocksdale
TITLE: Untitled bowl
MATERIALS: Blue gum eucalyptus
DIMENSIONS: 1³/₄"H x 4"Dia

The natural beauty of the wood
surface is amplified when presented
on a smaller form.

Photos: Photocraft

ARTIST: Kip Christensen
TITLE: Lidded jewelry bowl
MATERIALS: Elk antler, turquoise,
pink ivory wood
DIMENSIONS: 1³/₄"H x 3⁵/₈"Dia

Kip Christensen

ARTIST: David Sengel
TITLE: Lidded container
MATERIALS: Holly, rose thorns
and black lacquer
DIMENSIONS: 3¹/₂"H x 3¹/₂"Dia

Hans Weissflog

ARTIST: Hans Weissflog
TITLE: Ballbox
MATERIALS: Blackwood and boxwood
DIMENSIONS: 2"H x 2"Dia

Hans Weissflog is driven by the challenge of
designing and creating his intricate forms. He
increases the difficulty in producing his work
by utilizing two contrasting woods.

Photo: Roger Schreiber

ARTIST: Michael Peterson
TITLE: Bird Form
MATERIALS: Locust burl
DIMENSIONS: 4"H x 4"Dia

"While working with material and mass, surface and texture, color and form, I enjoy the tactile quality the small scale allows and how it is best discovered and read through the hands," Michael Peterson says. *Bird Form* is turned, carved, sandblasted and bleached.

Derek Bencomo

ARTIST: Derek Bencomo
TITLE: Keiki Valley #2
MATERIALS: Maple burl
DIMENSIONS: 6"H x 6"Dia

Photo: Tony Novak-Clifford

Frank Amigo

Photo: Vince Lupo

ARTIST: Frank Amigo
TITLE: Small Flower
MATERIALS: Silver maple
DIMENSIONS: 4³/₄"H x 5¹/₂"Dia

The bowl is carved in a manner reminiscent of natural forms, creating an ideal canvas to showcase the beauty of the wood.

ARTIST: Melvin Lindquist
TITLE: Sung Vase
MATERIALS: Curly myrtle
DIMENSIONS: 12"H x 5½"Dia

CONTRIBUTING ARTISTS

Ray Allen
Arizona
Pages 70, 71

Frank Amigo
Maryland
Page 125

Gianfranco Angelino
ITALY
Pages 61, 69

Derek Bencomo
Hawaii
Page 124

Christian Burchard
Oregon
Pages 21, 31

Kip Christensen
Utah
Pages 110, 120

Robert J. Cutler
Alaska
Pages 58, 68

Virginia Dotson
Arizona
Page 92

Dennis Elliott
Florida
Page 98

David Ellsworth
Pennsylvania
Pages 12, 103, 108

Jean-François Escoulen
FRANCE
Page 74

J. Paul Fennell
Arizona
Page 34

Melvyn Firmager
ENGLAND
Page 46

Ron Fleming
Oklahoma
Pages 14, 32, 41

Paul Fletcher
ENGLAND
Page 75

Clay Foster
Texas
Page 49

Giles Gilson
New York
Pages 11, 38, 72

David Groth
California
Page 40

Louise Hibbert
WALES
Page 57

Stephen Hogbin
CANADA
Pages 13, 42

Michelle Holzapfel
Vermont
Pages 15, 37, 53

Robyn Horn
Arkansas
Back cover, 14, 82, 95

Michael Hosaluk
CANADA
Pages 2-3, 51

Todd Hoyer
Arizona
Pages 14, 83, 104

Stephen Hughes
AUSTRALIA
Pages 47, 99, 106

William Hunter
California
Front cover, 1, 11, 86

Gary Johnson
Missourri
Page 60

Ray Jones
North Carolina
Page 63

John Jordan
Tennessee
Pages 13, 19, 50

Ron Kent
Hawaii
Pages 13, 26

Ray Key
ENGLAND
Page 27

Dan Kvitka
Oregon
Page 22

Stoney Lamar
North Carolina
Pages 14, 81, 85

Bud Latven
New Mexico
Page 73

Michael Lee
Hawaii
Page 56

Mark Lindquist
Florida
Pages 8, 29, 80

Melvin Lindquist
Florida
Pages 10, 126

Steve Loar
New York
Page 93

Craig Lossing
Minnesota
Page 111

Bert Marsh
ENGLAND
Page 30

Terry Martin
AUSTRALIA
Page 45

Hugh McKay
Oregon
Page 96

John Dodge Meyer
Georgia
Pages 20, 28

Johannes Michelsen
Vermont
Page 116

Connie Mississippi
California
Page 88

Bruce Mitchell
California
Page 25

Michael Mode
Vermont
Page 76

Gael Montgomerie
NEW ZEALAND
Page 39

William Moore
Oregon
Pages 6, 65, 94

Ed Moulthrop
Georgia
Pages 10, 23

Philip Moulthrop
Georgia
Pages 66, 67

Rolly Munro
NEW ZEALAND
Page 89

Dale Nish
Utah
Page 12

Liam O' Neill
IRELAND
Page 18

Rude Osolnik
Kentucky
Pages 11, 64, 100

Stephen Paulsen
California
Page 77

Michael Peterson
Washington
Pages 15, 36, 123

Andrew Potocnik
AUSTRALIA
Pages 114, 115

Gene Pozzesi
California
Page 35

James Prestini
Deceased
Pages 4, 9

Richard Raffan
AUSTRALIA
Pages 12, 118

Margaret Salt
AUSTRALIA
Page 99

Gary Sanders
Texas
Page 107

Jon Sauer
California
Pages 112, 113

Merryll Saylan
California
Page 90

Betty Scarpino
Indiana
Page 87

Mike Scott
WALES
Pages 55, 102

David Sengel
North Carolina
Pages 52, 97, 109, 121

Mark Sfirri
Pennsylvania
Pages 84, 93

Mike Shuler
California
Page 62

Jack Slentz
Arkansas
Page 78

Hayley Smith
WALES
Pages 48, 54

Al Stirt
Vermont
Page 54

Bob Stocksdale
California
Back cover, 10, 24, 119

Jack Straka
Hawaii
Pages 16, 101

Del Stubbs
Minnesota
Page 12

Frank Sudol
CANADA
Page 44

Ben Trupperbäumer
AUSTRALIA
Page 91

Hans Weissflog
GERMANY
Back cover, 43, 54, 122

Vic Wood
AUSTRALIA
Page 117

ACKNOWLEDGMENTS

The authors would like to thank Toni Sikes, whose vision and enthusiasm made this project happen, and Katie Kazan, our editor, for her patience and guidance. Our tireless and understanding staff — Chris Drosse, Kirsten Muenster, Sheryl Wallace, Sioux Ashe, Miki Leier and Habiba Fender — gave us the time and space we needed to complete this book. David Peters' outstanding photography captured the excitement of the work. Thanks also go to Hap Sakwa for his generous technical support, Mark and Kathy Lindquist for their input and perspective, and Jo Lauria and Tran Turner for their invaluable advice.

Our very special thanks for their encouragement and assistance go to: Robyn and John Horn, Jane and Arthur Mason, Mari and Irving Lipton, Ruth and David Waterbury, Fleur and Charles Bresler, Anita and Ron Wornick, Ruth Greenberg, Susan Steinhauser and Daniel Greenberg, Nancy and David Trautenberg, Doris and Harry Wolin, Dorothy and George Saxe, Joy and Allan Nachman, Linda Faber-Brickman and Arnold Brickman, Nancy and David Wolf, Bob Bohlen, Ken Spitzbard, Rick Cigel, Forrest Merrill and Edward Jacobson.

Most importantly, our thanks go to all the artists for creating and sharing their work with us. It continues to capture our imaginations and inspire us.